Fun Holiday Crafts
Kids Can Do!

Thanksgiving Day Crafts

Arlene and
Herbert Erlbach

Enslow Elementary
an imprint of
Enslow Publishers, Inc.
40 Industrial Road   PO Box 38

E

http://www.enslow.com

Introduction

The fourth Thursday in November is a special date to people in the United States of America. It is Thanksgiving. It is the day when people get together with their family and friends to give thanks. It is also a time to remember the Pilgrims' first harvest in 1621.

Thanksgiving did not become an annual American holiday for many years after the Pilgrims' first Thanksgiving. During colonial times, days of thanksgiving were celebrated when there were good harvests and other happy events. George Washington declared a day of Thanksgiving be observed on November 26, 1789. In the years that followed, many states had Thanksgiving celebrations.

The tradition of observing Thanksgiving as a national holiday on the fourth Thursday

in November did not happen until 1863. A magazine editor named Sarah Josepha Hale is mostly responsible for this idea. She wrote about Thanksgiving for almost forty years in magazines of the time. She sent letters to governors and presidents. President Abraham Lincoln proclaimed this date as a national day to give thanks, and we continue to celebrate it today.

In this book, you will discover many crafts to make your Thanksgiving special. You can use them for decorations or to give as Thanksgiving gifts. As you make them, think about the many people and things in your life for which you are thankful.

Miniature Pilgrims

These Pilgrims have empty film canisters for their bodies. Make a Pilgrim boy and girl to decorate your Thanksgiving table.

What You Will Need (for two pilgrims):

- scissors
- cotton swab
- red crayon or marker
- glue
- wiggle eyes

- film canisters
- sheets of black, white, pink, and brown construction paper
- yarn

1. Cut black construction paper into two strips, each 2- by 4-inches. Glue one of the 2- by 4- inch strips to each film canister. Trim, if necessary.

2. Cut two more strips from the black paper. These strips should measure 1- by 3-inches. Glue the middle of each strip to the back of each canister to form the Pilgrim's arms.

3. Cut construction paper to form heads and small round circles for hands. Glue on wiggle eyes and draw a smile on each. Attach the heads and hands to the canisters with glue.

4. Cut white paper to form the boy's collar. (You can use the pattern on page 27.) Glue it to the boy's coat.

5. Trace the pattern on page 27 for the boy's hat. Cut 1¾ inch long by ½ inch high black construction paper for brim. Glue together. Draw glitter "buckle" on front of hat.

6. Cut two pieces of white paper to form the girl's cap and apron. Attach the apron and cap with glue. Add yarn, or cut paper fringe for hair. Let dry.

Wrap the black paper around the film canisters . . .

Add the arms . . .

The hands and faces are next . . .

Your pilgrims are ready for the table!

Rocking Miniature Mayflower

This Mayflower rocks when you tap an end with your finger. You can use it as a centerpiece with the miniature Pilgrims.

What You Will Need:

- scissors
- paper plate
- pencil
- brown and white construction paper
- glue
- craft sticks
- crayons or markers

1. Place a folded plate on the brown paper. Draw two half circles on the paper around the paper plate.

2. Cut out both half-circles. Do not cut the plate. Use a crayon or marker to draw lines that will look like wood on the construction paper. Set the half-circles aside.

3. Use the sail patterns on page 27 to draw sails on the white paper. Cut them out.

4. On the main sail, print "Happy Thanksgiving" or other Thanksgiving messages.

5. Cut a small strip of white paper to form the ship's flag.

6. Glue one stick to the center and one stick to each end of the paper plate halves. This way your ship will balance.

7. Glue one of the brown paper half-circles over the side of the plate with the craft sticks glued to it. Glue the second half-circle to the other side of the plate.

8. Attach the sails to the craft sticks with glue.

9. When your *Mayflower* is dry, tap the edges. It will rock like a ship on the stormy sea.

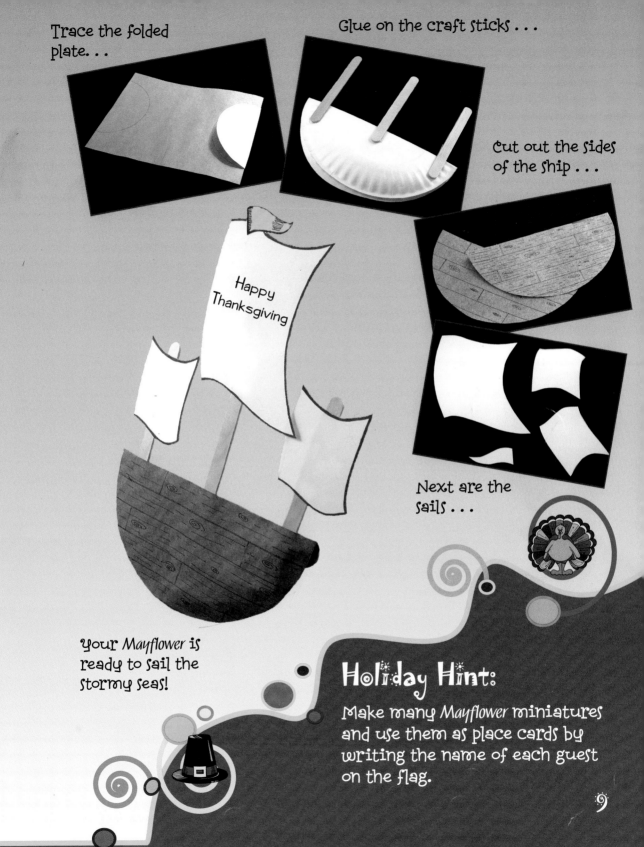

Trace the folded plate...

Glue on the craft sticks...

Cut out the sides of the ship...

Happy Thanksgiving

Next are the sails...

Your Mayflower is ready to sail the stormy seas!

Holiday Hint:

Make many Mayflower miniatures and use them as place cards by writing the name of each guest on the flag.

Beaded Corn Pin or Magnet

Corn is one of the crops that American Indians taught the Pilgrims how to plant. Make a corn pin or corn magnet to celebrate this important crop.

What You Will Need:

- scissors
- yellow, orange, and green pony beads or tri-beads
- cotton swab
- pipe cleaners cut into 6-inch pieces
- brown construction paper
- craft glue
- ribbon or yarn in a contrasting color
- a pin backing or magnetic tape

1. String eight beads onto each piece of pipe cleaner to form corncobs. Leave about a ¼-inch of pipe cleaner on the bottom of each cob. Leave about 1 inch on the top.

2. Fold a ¼-inch portion of pipe cleaner over the corncobs. Dab on glue to attach the folded portion of the pipe cleaner to the corn. This will hold the beads together on the bottom.

3. Twist the pipe cleaners on top as shown to hold the cobs of corn together on the top.

4. Cut construction paper into 4- by 4-inch pieces and fold it to create the husk. Glue it to the top of the corncobs.

5. Add ribbon or yarn.

6. Attach magnetic tape to the back of the corn to make a magnet. Glue on a pin backing to make a pin to wear.

Slide beads onto the pipe cleaners. . .

Twist the pipe cleaners together. . .

Display the beaded corn for all your family and friends to see!

Holiday Hint:

Wear your corn pin or use it as a refrigerator magnet.

Fall Tree Collage

A collage is a design made by pasting paper, cloth, and other things in an arrangement on a surface. This tree collage features brightly colored leaves made from tissue paper.

What You Will Need:

- scissors
- glue
- a paper edger (optional)
- pencil

- black, brown, and orange construction paper
- tissue paper in fall colors

1. Draw a tree on the brown paper. (You can use the pattern on page 28.) Cut out the tree.

2. Glue the tree to the black paper. Tear and cut tissue paper to form the leaves.

3. Glue your leaves onto the tree branches. Glue some of the leaves so they look like they are falling, or have fallen, to the ground. Let dry.

4. When your collage is complete, cut around the edge of your paper. A paper edger, if you have one, creates an attractive effect. Glue the collage to a sheet of orange paper.

Safety Note: Be sure to ask for help from an adult, if needed, to complete these crafts!

Draw a tree. . .

Carefully cut it out . . .

Glue it on another paper and add the leaves. . .

Your collage is ready for display!

Holiday Hint:

You can hang your tree collage on your front door as a welcome sign for Thanksgiving.

Leaves in the Wind Glitter Globe

In many parts of the country, trees have lost their leaves by November. Make your own leaf globe.

What You Will Need:

- newspaper to protect your workspace
- scissors
- large, clean, and dry baby food jars with lids. Remove the labels.
- cotton swabs
- fabric in a fall color
- pencil
- silicon-based (waterproof) glue
- water
- glitter
- foil confetti in leaf shapes
- baby oil (optional)

1. Place the jar's lid on the fabric. Draw around the lid of the jar with the pencil. Cut it out and set it aside. This will be the lid's covering.

2. Fill your jar with water. Add the baby oil if you plan to use it. The oil will make the leaves flow more slowly in the jar.

3. Add about ten confetti leaves to the jar.

4. Add a pinch of glitter. Be careful not to add too much glitter, or you will not be able to see the leaves flow through the jar.

5. Dab the glue around the inside of the lid with the cotton swab. Screw the lid on securely. Make sure that the jar is shut tightly. Dry overnight.

6. Glue the cut fabric to the top of the lid. Let dry.

7. Dab glue around the edge of the lid with a cotton swab. You may want to glue some glitter and pieces of confetti on the top. Let dry.

8. Shake your glitter globe and watch the leaves flutter and float.

First, make the
lid cover . . .

Add the confetti leaves
and glitter . . .

Glue the lid closed
and glue on the
fabric cover . . .

Give it a good shake
and watch the glitter
and leaves float
around!

Holiday Hint:

Make a glitter globe as a
present for someone that
you are grateful to have
in your life.

Leaf Plaque

You will use the dry brush technique of painting to create the leaf on your plaque.

What You Will Need:

- newspaper
- paper plate
- paintbrush
- brown construction paper
- pencil

- tissue paper
- hole punch
- glue
- scissors
- poster paint in fall colors like orange and yellow

- plastic bowls
- a leaf (optional)
- yarn or ribbon
- white paper
- scrap paper

1. Cover your worktable with newspaper.

2. Cover the paper plate with tissue paper. This will be the background for your painted leaf. Punch a hole at the top and set it aside.

3. Trace a leaf on the brown paper or use the pattern on page 26. Cut it out.

4. Pour paint into bowls. Dip your paintbrush into one color. Make brush strokes on the scrap paper until the paintbrush is almost dry. Brush the color onto the edges of your leaf. Wash your brush. Dip your paint into another color and repeat. You can brush colors over colors, if you like.

5. When you are satisfied with your dry brush leaf, let it dry completely. Then glue it to the paper plate background.

6. Loop the yarn through the hole. Your leaf plaque is ready to display.

Cover the paper plate with tissue paper . . .

Trace the leaf and cut it out . . .

Paint the leaf fall colors . . .

Add some yarn at the top and your plaque is ready to be hung up!

Holiday Hint:

You may wish to make several leaf plaques to hang throughout your house.

Scarecrow

Farmers place scarecrows in cornfields to frighten hungry birds away from their crops. This scarecrow will not scare anybody. You can wear it, use it as a magnet, or use it as a decoration.

What You Will Need:

- scissors
- fine-tipped marker
- cotton swab
- scraps of fabric or paper
- brown or yellow construction paper
- craft glue
- craft spoon
- craft sticks
- straw (optional)
- wiggle eyes
- magnetic tape or a pin backing

1. Glue the craft stick to the center of the craft spoon as shown. This will form the scarecrow's body.

2. Trace a hat, shirt, and pants onto construction paper. You can use the patterns on page 26. Cut them out. Glue shirt and pants to the scarecrow's body.

3. Glue on the wiggle eyes, and draw the scarecrow's mouth with the marker. Add the hat.

4. Glue the straw or cut paper to scarecrow's clothing.

5. Add pin backing to make a pin to wear. Add magnetic tape to make a magnet.

Glue the sticks together and then glue on the shirt and pants . . .

Next comes the hat and face . . .

Your scarecrow is ready to wear!

Holiday Hint:

Add the scarecrow to your other Thanksgiving decorations.

Pumpkin Napkin Rings

Pumpkins are a popular Thanksgiving decoration. Pumpkin was eaten by the Pilgrims at the first Thanksgiving. Make some pumpkin napkin rings to celebrate the season.

What You Will Need (for four napkin rings):

- scissors
- a toilet paper roll
- green and orange felt
- pipe cleaners
- tacky glue
- ric-rac (optional)

1. Squeeze the toilet paper roll flat and cut it into 1-inch sections.

2. Cut the orange felt into circles. These will be your pumpkins.

3. Cut the pipe cleaners into 2-inch pieces. Glue a piece of pipe cleaner onto the back of each pumpkin so that the stem sticks up over the pumpkin.

4. Cut the green felt into 1½- by 6-inch strips. Glue each strip to a piece of toilet paper roll. Fold the excess edges inside the paper roll and glue. Add ric-rac if desired. Let dry.

5. Glue the pumpkins to the napkin rings. Let dry.

Carefully cut up the toilet paper roll . . .

Make the pumpkins for the front . . .

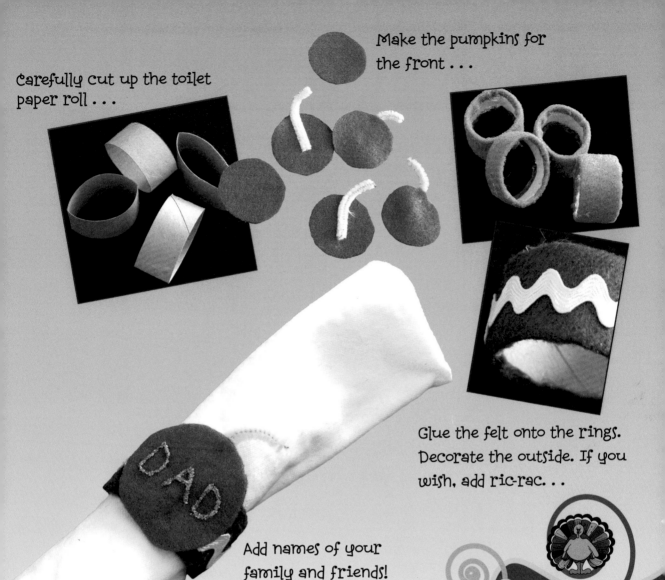

Glue the felt onto the rings. Decorate the outside. If you wish, add ric-rac. . .

Add names of your family and friends!

DAD

Holiday Hint:

Use your napkin rings at your Thanksgiving table.

21

Thankfulness Book

Think about the people and things for which you are thankful. Write about them in this book. You can illustrate it, too.

What You Will Need:

- scissors
- construction paper in orange and another color
- paper edger (optional)

- hole punch
- green pipe cleaners
- yarn or ribbon in a fall color
- white paper
- glue

- stickers, glitter, and/or bits of Thanksgiving confetti
- crayons
- pen or pencil

1. Cut two sheets of construction paper into 6- by 9-inch pieces. These will be the covers of your book. Cut a pumpkin shape from the orange paper. Add the pipe cleaner to make a stem for your pumpkin.

2. Decorate the cover with stickers, glitter, and Thanksgiving confetti. You can cut out your own designs and glue them on, too. Glue on yarn or ribbon to form a border.

3. Line up the sheets of paper that form the cover of your book. Punch holes so that they match. Punch the white paper to match the holes. You may need adult help for this. Poke the yarn or ribbon through the holes and tie.

4. Write about something that you are thankful for on each page. Draw pictures to illustrate your thoughts.

Glue a pumpkin to the front cover. . .

Decorate the cover with stickers, glitter, confetti, and other items . . .

Add blank pages inside and tie together with yarn . . .

Your book is ready for all your special thoughts!

Holiday Hint:

Give your Thankfulness Book to a family member or friend or read it aloud at Thanksgiving dinner.

Turkey Place Cards

These turkeys will show Thanksgiving guests where to sit at your holiday table.

What You Will Need (for each place card):

- scissors
- cupcake liners
- fine-tipped marker
- craft spoons

- index cards
- glue
- brown construction paper

- wiggle eyes
- scraps of red and orange paper.

1. Glue the cupcake liners so that they overlap, as shown.

2. Trace onto red and orange paper the turkey's wattle and beak. You can use the pattern on page 26. Cut them out. Glue them to the craft spoon. Add the wiggle eyes. Let dry.

3. Cut out a half-circle from the brown construction paper for the turkey's body. Glue to bottom of spoon.

4. Write a guest's name on the craft spoon.

5. Cut the index card in half and fold it to form a stand for the place card. Glue it to the back of the turkey. Let dry.

Glue together two cupcake liners . . .

Decorate the turkey head . . .

Add the names of the guests coming for dinner and your place card is ready!

Holiday Hint:

Make a Turkey place card for each guest and place them on your Thanksgiving table to make it festive.

Patterns

Use tracing paper to copy the patterns on these pages. Ask an adult to help you cut and trace the shapes onto construction paper.

Safety Note: Be sure to ask for help from an adult, if needed, to complete these crafts!

hat

shirt

pants

Scarecrow at 100%

Leaf at 100%

Turkey beak and wattle at 100%

Pilgrim clothes at 100%

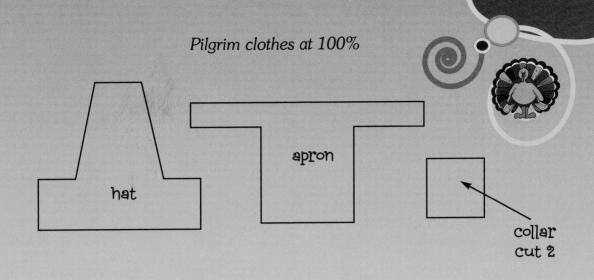

hat

apron

collar
cut 2

Mayflower
sails at 100%

main sail

smaller sail
cut 2

flag

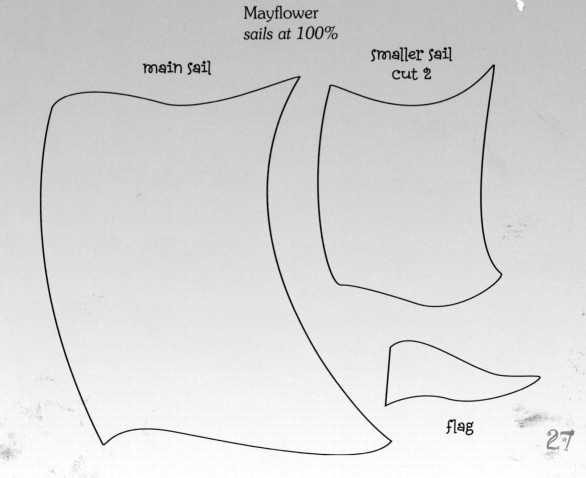

Enlarge tree by 160%

28

Words to Know

harvest—A gathering in of crops when they are ripe.

hull—The sides and bottom of a ship.

Mayflower—The ship that carried the first Pilgrims to America in 1620.

Pilgrims—The people who started a colony at Plymouth in New England in 1620.

scarecrow—A figure of a person used to frighten birds away from crops.

Thanksgiving—A holiday in the United States celebrated on the fourth Thursday in November to remember the first Pilgrims' harvest feast held in 1621.

tradition—The handing down of customs from parents to their children.

wattle—The skin that hangs from a turkey's neck.

Reading About Thanksgiving Day

Anderson, Laurie Halse. *Thank You, Sara: The Woman Who Saved Thanksgiving.* New York: Simon & Schuster Books for Young Readers, 2002.

Arnosky, Jim. *All About Turkeys.* New York: Scholastic Press, 1998.

Landau, Elaine. *Thanksgiving: A Time to Be Thankful.* Berkeley Heights, N.J.: Enslow Publishers, Inc., 2001.

Roop, Connie and Peter. *Let's Celebrate Thanksgiving.* Brookfield, Conn.: Millbrook Press, 1999.

Rosinsky, Natalie M. *Thanksgiving.* Minneapolis, Minn.: Compass Point Books, 2003.

Schuh, Mari C. *Thanksgiving Day.* Mankato, Minn.: Pebble Books, 2003.

Swamp, Chief Jake. *Giving Thanks: A Native American Good Morning Message.* New York: Lee & Low Books, 1995.

Internet Addresses

Thanksgiving on the Net

Learn even more about Thanksgiving from this Web site.

<http://www.holidays.net/thanksgiving/>

Holiday Fun: Thanksgiving Clip Art

Need some ideas for your Thanksgiving Day crafts?
Try this Web site.

<http://www.kidsdomain.com/holiday/thanks/
clipart.html>

Index